ACTIVITIES

Karl Nordvall
Contributing Writer: Mary Chadwick

Activity Book

Contents

SECTION 1 — New Neighbors

DAY	1	Introductions	5
DAY	2	The Visit	6
DAY	3	Occupations	7
DAY	4	School	8
DAY	5	Saying Goodbye	9

SECTION 2 — Shopping

DAY	6	Women's Clothing	11
DAY	7	Sizes and Trying Things On	12
DAY	8	Men's Clothing	13
DAY	9	Paying at the Counter	14
DAY	10	Electronics	15

SECTION 3 — Social Time

DAY	11	At a Fast Food Restaurant	17
DAY	12	At the Movies	18
DAY	13	Helping a Neighbor	19
DAY	14	At a Coffee Shop	20
DAY	15	At the Museum	21

SECTION 4 — Around the Town

DAY	16	Taking a Taxi	23
DAY	17	In the Library	24
DAY	18	Taking a Bus	25
DAY	19	Getting Gas	26
DAY	20	Asking for Directions	27

SECTION 5 — Restaurant

DAY	21	Arriving at the Restaurant	29
DAY	22	Ordering Drinks and an Appetizer	30
DAY	23	The Waiter Returns	31
DAY	24	The Food Arrives	32
DAY	25	A Lovely Meal	33

Contents

Airport

SECTION 6

DAY 26	Check-in	35
DAY 27	Security	36
DAY 28	Boarding	37
DAY 29	The Flight	38
DAY 30	Immigration (Arrival)	39

Travel

SECTION 7

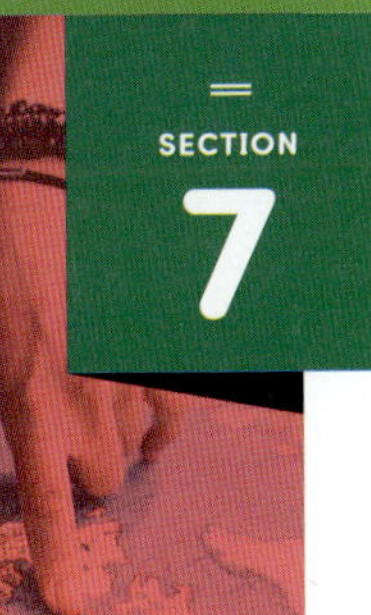

DAY 31	Car Rental	41
DAY 32	Hotel Check-In	42
DAY 33	The Hotel Concierge	43
DAY 34	Sightseeing	44
DAY 35	Hotel Check-out	45

Health

SECTION 8

DAY 36	Exercise	47
DAY 37	An Accident	48
DAY 38	In the Doctor's Office	49
DAY 39	The Examination	50
DAY 40	At the Pharmacy	51

Special Occasions

SECTION 9

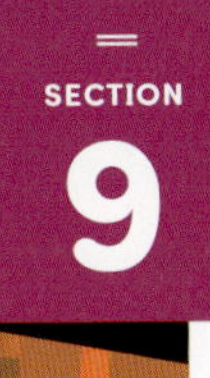

DAY 41	Planning a Party	53
DAY 42	Other Plans	54
DAY 43	Party Preparation	55
DAY 44	Wrapping a Gift	56
DAY 45	At the Party	57

Descriptions

SECTION 10

DAY 46	Getting a Haircut	59
DAY 47	Lost and Found	60
DAY 48	A Cooking Lesson	61
DAY 49	The Date	62
DAY 50	A Movie Discussion	63

Answer Key 64

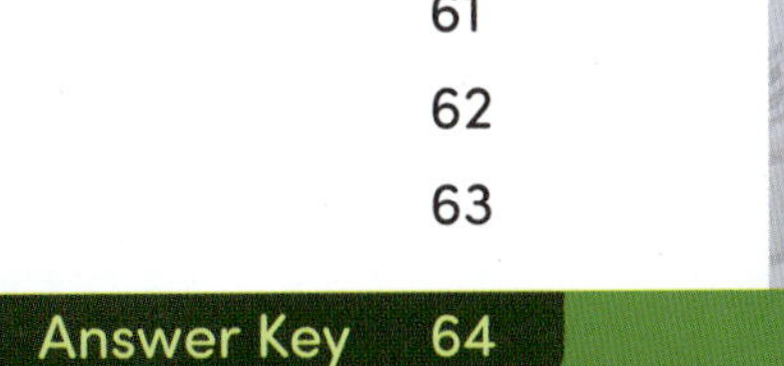

New Neighbors

새로운 이웃 만나기

DAY 1

소개
Introductions

SENTENCE PRACTICE

다양한 상황에서 표현을 연습하세요.

1. Please call me Sandy.

Janet Janet	**Matthew** Matthew
Frank Frank	**Wendy** Wendy

2. Trenton is my hometown.

Glasgow 글래스고	**Queensland** 퀸즐랜드
Halifax 핼리팩스	**Dover** 도버

3. What are your plans next week?

tomorrow morning 내일 아침	**next weekend** 다음 주
Tuesday night 화요일 밤	**this Sunday** 이번 주 일요일

4. Is around 7:00 OK?

8:00 8시	**4 p.m.** 오후 4시
2 o'clock 2시	**half past 5** 5시 30분

MINI DIALOGUE

우리말 부분을 영어로 적고 대화를 익혀 보세요.

1.

2.

DAY 2

방문
The Visit

SENTENCE PRACTICE

SENTENCE PRACTICE

한글 문장을 3초 안에 영어로 말하고 영어 문장을 써보세요.

1. 전화 주셔서 고마워요.　　　　Thanks for ____ .

2. 도와주셔서 고마워요.　　　　Thanks for ____ .

3. 당신의 모자를 받아드릴까요?　　May I take ____ ?

4. 당신의 가방들을 받아드릴까요?　May I take ____ ?

5. 부엌으로 가시죠.　　　　　Let's go into ____ .

6. 사무실로 가시죠.　　　　　Let's go into ____ .

7. 음료수 드릴까요?　　　　　Would you like ____ ?

8. 먹을 것 좀 드릴까요?　　　Would you like ____ ?

calling 전화	**helping** 도움	**your hat** 당신의 모자	**your bags** 당신의 가방들
the kitchen 부엌	**the office** 사무실	**a drink** 음료수	**something to eat** 먹을 것

MINI DIALOGUE

우리말 부분을 영어로 적고 대화를 익혀 보세요.

1.

2.

DAY 3

직업
Occupations

SENTENCE PRACTICE

배운 표현을 5번 크게 읽고 빈칸에 써보세요.

1. How do you like Dallas? 댈러스가 마음에 드세요?

따라 읽기 ① ② ③ ④ ⑤

____

2. How do you like Sydney? 시드니가 마음에 드세요?

따라 읽기 ① ② ③ ④ ⑤

____

3. I work for a marketing firm. 저는 마케팅 회사에서 일해요.

따라 읽기 ① ② ③ ④ ⑤

____

4. I work for a publishing company. 저는 출판사에서 일해요.

따라 읽기 ① ② ③ ④ ⑤

____

5. I'm an English teacher. 저는 영어 선생님이에요.

따라 읽기 ① ② ③ ④ ⑤

____

6. I'm a lawyer. 저는 변호사예요.

따라 읽기 ① ② ③ ④ ⑤

____

MINI DIALOGUE

우리말 부분을 영어로 적고 대화를 익혀 보세요.

1.

2.

DAY 4

학교
School

배운 표현을 5번 크게 읽고 빈칸에 써보세요.

1. **I majored in psychology.** 저는 심리학을 전공했어요.
   따라 읽기 ① ② ③ ④ ⑤

   ____

2. **I majored in engineering.** 저는 공학을 전공했어요.
   따라 읽기 ① ② ③ ④ ⑤

   ____

3. **My sister is a freshman there.** 제 여동생이 거기 신입생입니다.
   따라 읽기 ① ② ③ ④ ⑤

   ____

4. **My brother is a senior there.** 제 남동생이 거기 4학년입니다.
   따라 읽기 ① ② ③ ④ ⑤

   ____

5. **May I use your notebook?** 당신의 공책을 써도 될까요?
   따라 읽기 ① ② ③ ④ ⑤

   ____

6. **May I use your pen?** 당신의 펜을 써도 될까요?
   따라 읽기 ① ② ③ ④ ⑤

   ____

MINI DIALOGUE

우리말 부분을 영어로 적고 대화를 익혀 보세요.

1.

2.

DAY 5

작별 인사
Saying Goodbye

SENTENCE PRACTICE

한글 문장을 3초 안에 영어로 말하고 영어 문장을 써보세요.

1. 물 좀 드릴까요?　　　　　　　Can I get you __________________________________?

2. 담요를 드릴까요?　　　　　　　Can I get you __________________________________?

3. 새 포크를 드릴게요.　　　　　　I'll get you __________________________________.

4. 종이를 좀 드릴게요.　　　　　　I'll get you __________________________________.

5. 당신과 만나서 기뻤어요.　　　　It was _________________ to _________________ you.

6. 당신과 이야기해서 정말 좋았어요.　It was very _________________ to _________________ to you.

7. 당신이 오후에 시간이 있기를 바랍니다.　I hope __________________________________.

8. Theo가 올 수 있기를 바랍니다.　　I hope __________________________________.

---

some water 물 조금	**a blanket** 담요	**a new fork** 새 포크	**some paper** 약간의 종이
nice 좋은, 기쁜	**meet** 만나다	**talk** 이야기하다	
you have time in the afternoon 당신이 오후에 시간이 있다			
Theo can come over Theo가 올 수 있다			

MINI DIALOGUE

우리말 부분을 영어로 적고 대화를 익혀 보세요.

1.

2.

SECTION
2
Shopping
쇼핑하기

DAY 6

여성복
Women's Clothing

SENTENCE PRACTICE

다양한 상황에서 표현을 연습하세요.

1. I'm looking for some winter clothes.

some fall clothes 가을옷	**a suit** 정장
a leather jacket 가죽 재킷	**a pink shirt** 핑크색 셔츠

2. What color coat would you like?

size 크기	**sweater** 스웨터
length 길이	**shorts** 반바지

3. How about this dress?

this blouse 이 블라우스	**these jeans** 이 청바지
this bag 이 가방	**this color** 이 색상

4. Would you like to see these in a larger size?

go shopping with me 나와 함께 쇼핑을 하러 가다	**try this skirt on** 스커트를 입어보다

MINI DIALOGUE

우리말 부분을 영어로 적고 대화를 익혀 보세요.

1.

2.

DAY 7

사이즈와 입어보기
Sizes and Trying Things On

SENTENCE PRACTICE

다양한 상황에서 표현을 연습하세요.

1. I'd like these in pink.

all three of them 이것 세 개 다	**a smaller size** 작은 사이즈
a silk scarf 실크 스카프	**one of every color** 모든 색 하나씩

2. What colors do you wear?

size 사이즈	**brands** 상표
style 스타일	**clothes** 옷

3. Why don't you try this one first?

take a look at that one 저것을 보다	**put this one on** 이것을 입어보다
try on a bigger size 큰 사이즈를 입어보다	**get both of them** 둘 다 사다

4. They feel too tight.

uncomfortable 불편한	**thick** 두꺼운
too short 너무 짧은	**thin** 얇은

MINI DIALOGUE

우리말 부분을 영어로 적고 대화를 익혀 보세요.

1.

2.

DAY 8

남성복
Men's Clothing

SENTENCE PRACTICE

한글 문장을 3초 안에 영어로 말하고 영어 문장을 써보세요.

1. 저는 셔츠가 필요합니다.　　**I need** ____.

2. 저는 양말 몇 개가 필요합니다.　　**I need** ____.

3. 어떤 스타일의 스웨터를 찾으세요?　　**What** _____________ **of** _____________ **are you looking for?**

4. 어떤 종류의 재킷을 찾으세요?　　**What** _____________ **of** _____________ **are you looking for?**

5. 청남방 있나요?　　**Do you have** ____?

6. 실크 치마 있나요?　　**Do you have** ____?

7. 저것 두 개로 할게요.　　**I'll take** ____.

8. 더 큰 것으로 할게요.　　**I'll take** ____.

a shirt 셔츠	**some socks** 양말 몇 개	**style** 스타일	**sweater** 스웨터
kind 종류	**jacket** 재킷	**denim shirts** 청남방	**silk skirts** 실크 치마
two of those 저것 두 개	**the bigger one** 더 큰 것		

MINI DIALOGUE

우리말 부분을 영어로 적고 대화를 익혀 보세요.

1.

2.

DAY 9

카운터에서 계산하기
Paying at the Counter

SENTENCE PRACTICE

한글 문장을 3초 안에 영어로 말하고 영어 문장을 써보세요.

1. 총 9.50 달러에요.

Your total is ___________________________________.

2. 총 7,390.90 달러에요.

Your total is ___________________________________.

3. 이 쿠폰을 여기서 사용할 수 있을까요?

Can I use ___________________________________ here?

4. 여기서 신용카드를 사용할 수 있을까요?

Can I use ___________________________________ here?

5. 여기 당신의 카드가 있습니다.

Here's ___________________________________.

6. 여기 당신의 쿠폰이 있습니다.

Here's ___________________________________.

7. 저희와 통화가 필요하시면,
영수증 뒤편에 있는 번호로 전화주세요.

If you need to ___________________________________,
just use the number on the back of the receipt.

8. 큰 사이즈로 교환하고 싶으시면,
그냥 가져오세요.

If you need to ___________________________________,
just ___________________________________.

this coupon 이 쿠폰	**a credit card** 신용카드	**your card** 당신의 카드
your coupon 당신의 쿠폰	**call us** 우리에게 전화하다	
exchange this for a bigger size 큰 사이즈로 교환하다		**bring it back** 가져오다

MINI DIALOGUE

우리말 부분을 영어로 적고 대화를 익혀 보세요.

1.

2.

DAY 10

전자제품
Electronics

SENTENCE PRACTICE

다양한 상황에서 표현을 연습하세요.

1. Do you sell Bluetooth speakers?

USB cords USB 코드	**monitors** 모니터
keyboards 키보드	**computer software** 컴퓨터 소프트웨어

2. I'd like one that's easy to operate.

cheap 저렴한	**great for travel** 이동하기 편한
not too big 너무 크지 않은	**compact and lightweight** 소형이고 가벼운

3. It's made in Canada.

Japan 일본	**Vietnam** 베트남
China 중국	**the USA** 미국

4. This headphone set comes with a carrying case.

This laptop 이 노트북	**a charging cable** 충전 케이블
This cell phone 이 휴대폰	**free earphones** 무료 이어폰

MINI DIALOGUE

우리말 부분을 영어로 적고 대화를 익혀 보세요.

1.

2.

SECTION 3

Social Time

친구 만나기

DAY 11

패스트푸드점에서
At a Fast Food Restaurant

SENTENCE PRACTICE

한글 문장을 3초 안에 영어로 말하고 영어 문장을 써보세요.

1. 무엇을 드실래요?　　　　**What are you going to** _______________________?

2. 무엇을 드실 건가요?　　　**What are you going to** _______________________?

3. 물 좀 더 주시겠어요?　　　**Could I have** _______________________?

4. 여분의 냅킨을 주시겠어요?　**Could I have** _______________________?

5. 접시를 좀 가져갈게요.　　　**I'll get** _______________________.

6. 마요네즈를 좀 가져갈게요.　**I'll get** _______________________.

7. 버거는 다 드셨나요?　　　　**Are you finished with your** _______________________?

8. 식사는 다 드셨나요?　　　　**Are you finished with your** _______________________?

have 먹다	**eat** 먹다	**some more water** 물 조금 더
an extra napkin 여분의 냅킨	**some plates** 접시 몇 개	**some mayonnaise** 마요네즈 조금
burger 버거	**meal** 식사	

MINI DIALOGUE

우리말 부분을 영어로 적고 대화를 익혀 보세요.

1.

2.

DAY 12

극장에서
At the Movies

SENTENCE PRACTICE

대화를 보고 빈칸을 채워보세요.

1. **A** Which _________________ do you want to see?
   어떤 로맨스 영화를 볼래요?

   B What about *Flowers in Bloom*?
   '*Flowers in Bloom*' 어때요?

2. **A** Which _________________ do you want to see?
   어떤 액션 영화를 볼래요?

   B I'd like to see *Dawn of Revenge*.
   '*Dawn of Revenge*'를 보고 싶어요.

3. **A** Are there any good movies out right now?
   지금 재밌는 영화 상영하는 거 있나요?

   B I heard _________________ is good.
   '*Die Tomorrow*'가 좋다던데요.

4. **A** I heard _________________ is good.
   '*Blue Skies*'가 좋다던데요.

   B Oh, yeah? Let's go see that!
   오, 그래요? 그거 보러 가요!

romance movie 로맨스 영화	**action film** 액션 영화
Die Tomorrow Die Tomorrow	***Blue Skies*** Blue Skies

MINI DIALOGUE

우리말 부분을 영어로 적고 대화를 익혀 보세요.

1. 

2. 

DAY 13

이웃 돕기
Helping a Neighbor

SENTENCE PRACTICE

다양한 상황에서 표현을 연습하세요.

1. Let me get your coat **for you.**

take 가지고 가다	**your bag** 당신의 가방
carry 들다	**your jacket** 당신의 재킷

2. Where should I put these bags**?**

your luggage 당신의 짐	**these pots** 이 냄비들
your clothes 당신의 옷	**this box** 이 박스

3. Would you mind holding this for me**?**

picking that up for me 나를 위해 그것을 들다	**opening the window** 창문을 열다
getting the mail for me 나를 위해 편지를 가져오다	**mowing my lawn** 잔디를 깎다

4. I'm so glad to know you**.**

see you 당신을 보다	**have you here** 당신이 여기 있다
know you'll help me 당신이 나를 도와줄 것을 알다	**run into you** 당신을 우연히 만나다

MINI DIALOGUE

우리말 부분을 영어로 적고 대화를 익혀 보세요.

1.

2.

DAY 14

커피숍에서
At a Coffee Shop

SENTENCE PRACTICE

한글 문장을 3초 안에 영어로 말하고 영어 문장을 써보세요.

1. 해피 커피에 오신 것을 환영합니다.
   Welcome to ____.

2. 홈 팰리스에 오신 것을 환영합니다.
   Welcome to ____.

3. 핫 초콜릿으로 할게요.
   I'd like ____.

4. 작은 사이즈의 디카페인 커피로 할게요.
   I'd like _______________________________________, please.

5. 저기서 설탕과 우유를 받아 가세요.
   You can get _______________________________ over there.

6. 저기서 상품권을 받아 가세요.
   You can get _______________________________ over there.

7. 저에게 따뜻한 카푸치노를 주실래요?
   Can you get _______________________________ for me?

8. 저에게 크림을 좀 주실래요?
   Can you get _______________________________ for me?

Happy Coffee 해피 커피   **Home Palace** 홈 팰리스   **a hot chocolate** 핫 초콜릿

a small decaf 작은 사이즈의 디카페인 커피   **sugar and milk** 설탕과 우유   **a gift card** 상품권

a hot cappuccino 따뜻한 카푸치노   **some creams** 크림

MINI DIALOGUE

우리말 부분을 영어로 적고 대화를 익혀 보세요.

1.

2.

DAY 15

박물관에서
At the Museum

SENTENCE PRACTICE

다양한 상황에서 표현을 연습하세요.

1. That sounds good.

great 정말 좋은	**fun** 재미있는, 즐거운
interesting 흥미로운	**boring** 재미없는, 지루한

2. Are there English tours?

Chinese explanations 중국어 설명	**any special exhibits** 특별 전시
group tours 그룹 투어	**English explanations** 영문 설명

3. You can't talk here.

eat in here 여기서 먹다	**go in there** 거기 들어가다
talk loudly here 여기서 크게 이야기하다	**enter this exhibit** 그 전시관에 들어가다

4. What was your favorite part of the exhibition?

object 물건	**section** 구획
exhibit 전시품	**floor** 층

MINI DIALOGUE

우리말 부분을 영어로 적고 대화를 익혀 보세요.

1.

2.

SECTION
4
Around the Town
동네 한 바퀴 돌아다니기

DAY 16

택시 타기
Taking a Taxi

SENTENCE PRACTICE

배운 표현을 5번 크게 읽고 빈칸에 써보세요.

1. **Do you want to take the ferry or the subway?** 페리를 타실래요, 아니면 지하철을 타실래요?
   따라 읽기 ① ② ③ ④ ⑤

   ____

2. **Do you want to take a taxi?** 택시를 타실래요?
   따라 읽기 ① ② ③ ④ ⑤

   ____

3. **Let's take the subway.** 지하철을 탑시다.
   따라 읽기 ① ② ③ ④ ⑤

   ____

4. **Let's take the train.** 기차를 탑시다.
   따라 읽기 ① ② ③ ④ ⑤

   ____

5. **We are going to Jones' Headquarters.** 존스 본사로 갑시다.
   따라 읽기 ① ② ③ ④ ⑤

   ____

6. **We are going to Carnegie Park.** 카네기 공원으로 갑시다.
   따라 읽기 ① ② ③ ④ ⑤

MINI DIALOGUE

우리말 부분을 영어로 적고 대화를 익혀 보세요.

1. 

2. 

DAY 17

도서관에서
In the Library

SENTENCE PRACTICE

한글 문장을 3초 안에 영어로 말하고 영어 문장을 써보세요.

1. 저는 로맨스를 좋아해요.　　I love ___________________________.

2. 저는 전기를 좋아해요.　　I love ___________________________.

3. 'The Bluebird' 입니다.　　It's called ___________________________.

4. 'On the Hills' 입니다.　　It's called ___________________________.

5. 가장 좋아하는 화가가 누구예요?　　Who is your favorite ___________________________?

6. 가장 좋아하는 미스터리 작가가 누구예요?　　Who is your favorite ___________________________?

7. 그 시는 무슨 내용이에요?　　What's ___________________________ about?

8. 'Burning House'는 무슨 내용이에요?　　What's ___________________________ about?

romances 로맨스	**biographies** 전기	**The Bluebird** The Bluebird	**On the Hills** On the Hills
artist 화가	**mystery writer** 미스터리 작가	**the poem** 그 시	**Burning House** Burning House

MINI DIALOGUE

우리말 부분을 영어로 적고 대화를 익혀 보세요.

1.

2.

DAY 18

버스 타기
Taking a Bus

SENTENCE PRACTICE

다양한 상황에서 표현을 연습하세요.

1. Which bus goes to The Art Center?

Central Station 중앙역	**harbor** 항구
the library 도서관	**the art museum** 미술관

2. How often does the 343 bus come?

the bus to New Haven 뉴헤이븐으로 가는 버스	**the tram** 트램
the F train F 열차	**the hotel bus** 호텔 버스

3. It comes every 20 minutes.

every five minutes 5분마다	**four times a day** 하루에 네 번
once an hour 시간당 한 번	**twice an hour** 시간당 두 번

4. Kim gets on the 268.

James James	**the 487** 487번
He 그	**the tram** 전차

MINI DIALOGUE

우리말 부분을 영어로 적고 대화를 익혀 보세요.

1.

2.

DAY 19

주유하기
Getting Gas

SENTENCE PRACTICE

배운 표현을 5번 크게 읽고 빈칸에 써보세요.

1. **I should get some snacks.** 간식 좀 사야겠어요.
   따라 읽기 ① ② ③ ④ ⑤

   ____

2. **I should get some water.** 물 좀 마셔야겠어요.
   따라 읽기 ① ② ③ ④ ⑤

   ____

3. **It saves us the hassle.** 번거로움을 덜어줍니다.
   따라 읽기 ① ② ③ ④ ⑤

   ____

4. **It saves us time and trouble.** 시간과 노고가 덜어집니다.
   따라 읽기 ① ② ③ ④ ⑤

   ____

5. **Just mid-grade, please.** 중간등급으로요.
   따라 읽기 ① ② ③ ④ ⑤

   ____

6. **Just diesel, please.** 그냥 경유로요.
   따라 읽기 ① ② ③ ④ ⑤

   ____

MINI DIALOGUE

우리말 부분을 영어로 적고 대화를 익혀 보세요.

1.

DAY 20

길 묻기
Asking for Directions

SENTENCE PRACTICE

다양한 상황에서 표현을 연습하세요.

1. How can we get to the shoe store?

the library 도서관	**the high school** 고등학교
the fire station 소방서	**the office supply store** 사무용품 가게

2. Do you know where the post office is?

the supermarket 슈퍼마켓	**the gym** 체육관
the craft store 공예품점	**the clerk's office** 직원 사무실

3. Turn left and drive for two miles.

right at the light 신호에서 오른쪽으로

left and then drive a quarter of a mile 왼쪽으로 그리고 4분의 1마일 운전하다

right at the next corner 다음 모퉁이에서 오른쪽으로

left at the second light 두 번째 신호에서 왼쪽으로

4. It's on your back.

right by the pizza shop 피자 가게 옆 오른쪽

left across from the car dealership 자동차 판매점 건너 왼쪽

right next to the elementary school 초등학교 오른쪽 옆

left near the supermarket 슈퍼마켓 왼쪽 근처

MINI DIALOGUE

우리말 부분을 영어로 적고 대화를 익혀 보세요.

1.

2.

SECTION 5

Restaurant

레스토랑에서 식사하기

DAY 21

식당에서
Arriving at the Restaurant

SENTENCE PRACTICE

다양한 상황에서 표현을 연습하세요.

1. We have a reservation for 3:30.

4 o'clock 4시	**tomorrow night** 내일 저녁
5 p.m. 오후 5시	**2:30** 2시 30분

2. Will mashed potatoes be all right?

cherry coke 체리 맛 콜라	**this table** 이 테이블
steamed green beans 찐 완두콩	**this seat** 이 자리

3. Do you have a seat next to the bar?

a table 테이블	**the kitchen** 부엌
a spot 자리	**the windows** 창문

4. Jeanne will be with you shortly.

The waiter 웨이터	**soon** 곧
The manager 매니저	**in a moment** 바로

MINI DIALOGUE

우리말 부분을 영어로 적고 대화를 익혀 보세요.

1.

2.

음료와 애피타이저 주문
Ordering Drinks and an Appetizer

SENTENCE PRACTICE

배운 표현을 5번 크게 읽고 빈칸에 써보세요.

1. **Everything looks great!** 모든 것이 훌륭해 보이네요!
   따라 읽기 ① ② ③ ④ ⑤

   ____

2. **Everything looks amazing!** 모든 것이 좋아 보이네요!
   따라 읽기 ① ② ③ ④ ⑤

   ____

3. **Can I get you anything to eat?** 먹을 것 좀 가져다드릴까요?
   따라 읽기 ① ② ③ ④ ⑤

   ____

4. **Can I get you anything to munch on?** 씹을 것 좀 가져다드릴까요?
   따라 읽기 ① ② ③ ④ ⑤

   ____

5. **I will have french fries.** 감자튀김 주세요.
   따라 읽기 ① ② ③ ④ ⑤

   ____

6. **I will have the spaghetti and meatballs.** 스파게티와 미트볼 주세요.
   따라 읽기 ① ② ③ ④ ⑤

MINI DIALOGUE

우리말 부분을 영어로 적고 대화를 익혀 보세요.

1. 

2.

DAY 23

웨이터가 돌아오다
The Waiter Returns

한글 문장을 3초 안에 영어로 말하고 영어 문장을 써보세요.

1. 디저트 드시겠어요? Are you ready ____?

2. 가시겠어요? Are you ready ____?

3. 콩은 어떻게 해드릴까요? How would you like _________________________________?

4. 감자는 어떻게 해드릴까요? How would you like _________________________________?

5. 야채, 닭고기, 새우 타코가 있습니다. We have_______________, _______________, and _______________ tacos.

6. 모차렐라, 페퍼잭, 체다가 있습니다. We have _______________, _______________, and _______________.

7. 클럽 샌드위치에는 뭐가 들어가죠? What's in your _____________________________________?

8. 주방장의 샐러드에는 뭐가 들어가죠? What's in your _____________________________________?

for dessert 디저트로	**to go** 가다	**your beans** 당신의 콩	**your potatoes** 당신의 감자
veggie 야채	**chicken** 닭고기	**shrimp** 새우	**mozzarella** 모차렐라
pepperjack 페퍼잭	**cheddar** 체다	**club sandwich** 클럽 샌드위치	**chef's salad** 주방장의 샐러드

우리말 부분을 영어로 적고 대화를 익혀 보세요.

1.

DAY 24

음식이 도착하다
The Food Arrives

SENTENCE PRACTICE

한글 문장을 3초 안에 영어로 말하고 영어 문장을 써보세요.

1. 음식은 괜찮으세요?　　　Is ____ all right?

2. 음료는 괜찮으세요?　　　Is ____ all right?

3. 너무 차갑네요.　　　It's ____.

4. 적당하네요.　　　It's ____.

5. 여분의 접시를 드릴까요?　　　Would you like ____?

6. 다른 마실 것을 드릴까요?　　　Would you like ____?

7. 제가 당신의 빈 잔들을 치우겠습니다.　　　I'll take ____ away.

8. 제가 그 접시들을 치우겠습니다.　　　I'll take ____ away.

---

your food 당신의 음식　　　**your drink** 당신의 음료

too cold 너무 차가운　　　**just right** 적당한

an extra plate 여분의 접시　　　**something else to drink** 다른 마실 것

your empty glasses 당신의 빈 잔들　　　**those plates** 그 접시들

MINI DIALOGUE

우리말 부분을 영어로 적고 대화를 익혀 보세요.

1.

2.

DAY 25

맛있는 식사
A Lovely Meal

다양한 상황에서 표현을 연습하세요.

1. Could we have another drink**, please?**

a napkin 냅킨	**seat on the terrace** 테라스 자리
a few more minutes 몇 분 더	**another menu** 다른 메뉴

2. Here's your meal.

drink 음료	**soup** 수프
food 음식	**appetizer** 전채 요리

3. Could I take this drink home with me**?**

all of this 이것 다	**an extra dressing** 여분의 드레싱
this food 이 음식	**this pizza home** 이 피자를 집에

4. My parents **were satisfied with** everything**.**

My family 우리 가족	**the meal** 식사
My clients 우리 고객들	**the restaurant** 식당

우리말 부분을 영어로 적고 대화를 익혀 보세요.

1.

2.

SECTION 6

Airport

비행기 타고 내리기

DAY 26

탑승 수속
Check-in

SENTENCE PRACTICE

배운 표현을 5번 크게 읽고 빈칸에 써보세요.

1. **Can I see another form of ID, please?** 다른 유형의 신분증을 보여주실래요?
   따라 읽기 ① ② ③ ④ ⑤

   ____

2. **Can I see your return ticket, please?** 돌아오는 표를 보여주실래요?
   따라 읽기 ① ② ③ ④ ⑤

   ____

3. **Did you pack all of these bags yourself?** 이 모든 가방들을 다 직접 싸셨나요?
   따라 읽기 ① ② ③ ④ ⑤

   ____

4. **Did you pack your own bags?** 이 가방들을 직접 싸셨나요?
   따라 읽기 ① ② ③ ④ ⑤

   ____

5. **I'd like an aisle seat, please.** 통로 쪽 좌석으로 부탁합니다.
   따라 읽기 ① ② ③ ④ ⑤

   ____

6. **I'd like an emergency exit seat, please.** 비상구 좌석으로 부탁합니다.
   따라 읽기 ① ② ③ ④ ⑤

   ____

MINI DIALOGUE

우리말 부분을 영어로 적고 대화를 익혀 보세요.

1.

2.

DAY 27

보안 검색
Security

다양한 상황에서 표현을 연습하세요.

1. Please empty your son's pockets.

your purse 당신의 지갑	**that container** 그 용기
your bag 당신의 가방	**the water bottle** 물병

2. Can I look through your purse?

your bag 당신의 가방	**your things** 당신의 물건들
your suitcase 당신의 여행 가방	**your luggage** 당신의 수하물

3. They are pills for my liver.

inhalers 흡입기	**my asthma** 천식
blood thinners 혈액 희석제	**my heart** 심장

4. Please go to the next counter.

immigration 출국 심사대	**that officer over there** 저쪽에 있는 사무실
counter 8 8번 카운터	**gate 34** 34번 게이트

우리말 부분을 영어로 적고 대화를 익혀 보세요.

1.

2.

DAY 28

탑승
Boarding

한글 문장을 3초 안에 영어로 말하고 영어 문장을 써보세요.

1. 파리로 가는 309편 비행기 탑승을 시작하겠습니다.

We will now begin boarding ______________________________________.

2. 모든 줄 탑승을 시작하겠습니다.

We will now begin boarding ______________________________________.

3. 이 가방을 치워드릴까요?

Would you like me to ______________________________________?

4. 안전벨트 연장선을 가져다드릴까요?

Would you like me to ______________________________________?

5. 좌석 아래에 둘게요.

I'd like to ______________________________________.

6. 좌석 아래쪽에 둘게요.

I'd like to ______________________________________.

7. 모든 전자기기의 전원을 꺼주세요.

Please make sure ______________________________________.

8. 탁자를 다 접어주세요.

Please make sure ______________________________________.

---

for flight 309 to Paris 파리로 가는 309편 비행기

put this bag away for you 이 가방을 치우다

put this under my seat 이것을 좌석 아래 두다

all electronic devices are turned off 모든 전자기기의 전원을 끄다

all trays are put away 모든 탁자를 접다

all rows 모든 줄

get you a seat belt extender 안전벨트 연장선을 가져다주다

put this underneath my seat 이것을 좌석 아래쪽에 두다

우리말 부분을 영어로 적고 대화를 익혀 보세요.

1.

Excuse me, sir. Could I ______________________?
That's my seat by the window.
실례합니다, 선생님. 지나갈 수 있을까요? 창 쪽이 제 좌석이거든요.

2.

DAY 29

비행
The Flight

SENTENCE PRACTICE

배운 표현을 5번 크게 읽고 빈칸에 써보세요.

1. Is this your first time going abroad? 해외여행은 처음인가요?

따라 읽기 ① ② ③ ④ ⑤

____

2. Is this your first time on a plane? 비행기 탑승이 처음인가요?

따라 읽기 ① ② ③ ④ ⑤

____

3. I'm going to go sightseeing. 관광할 예정입니다.

따라 읽기 ① ② ③ ④ ⑤

____

4. I'm going to attend a language school. 어학원에 다닐 예정입니다.

따라 읽기 ① ② ③ ④ ⑤

____

5. Would you like to switch seats or stay in your seat? 자리를 바꾸실래요 아니면 그 자리에 계시겠어요?

따라 읽기 ① ② ③ ④ ⑤

____

6. Would you like to drink some coffee or have some tea? 커피와 차 중 어느 것으로 하시겠어요?

따라 읽기 ① ② ③ ④ ⑤

____

MINI DIALOGUE

우리말 부분을 영어로 적고 대화를 익혀 보세요.

1.

2.

DAY 30

입국심사 (도착)
Immigration (Arrival)

SENTENCE PRACTICE

한글 문장을 3초 안에 영어로 말하고 영어 문장을 써보세요.

1. 로마에서 왔습니다.　　I flew in from ___________________________________.

2. 브뤼셀에서 왔습니다.　　I flew in from ___________________________________.

3. 얼마 동안 가족을 방문하실 겁니까?　　How long will you be ___________________________?

4. 얼마 동안 여기 머무르실 겁니까?　　How long will you be ___________________________?

5. 이틀 동안 머무를 겁니다.　　I'll be here for just ___________________________.

6. 다음 두 달 동안 머무를 겁니다.　　I'll be here for ___________________________.

7. 여기 가족 일을 보러 왔습니다.　　I'm just here ___________________________.

8. 여기 친구를 만나러 왔습니다.　　I'm just here ___________________________.

Rome 로마	**Brussels** 브뤼셀	**visiting family** 가족 방문
here 여기	**two days** 이틀	**the next two months** 다음 두 달
on some family business 가족 일	**seeing a friend** 친구 만나기	

MINI DIALOGUE

우리말 부분을 영어로 적고 대화를 익혀 보세요.

1.

2.

SECTION 7

Travel

관광하며 돌아다니기

DAY 31

차 빌리기
Car Rental

SENTENCE PRACTICE

배운 표현을 5번 크게 읽고 빈칸에 써보세요.

1. **I'd like an SUV, please.** 스포츠 실용차로 할게요.
   따라 읽기 ① ② ③ ④ ⑤

   ____

2. **I'd like a minivan, please.** 미니밴으로 할게요.
   따라 읽기 ① ② ③ ④ ⑤

   ____

3. **I'll need it for three days.** 3일 동안 사용할게요.
   따라 읽기 ① ② ③ ④ ⑤

   ____

4. **I'll need it for two weeks.** 2주 동안 사용할게요.
   따라 읽기 ① ② ③ ④ ⑤

   ____

5. **Please show us your invoice.** 청구서를 보여주세요.
   따라 읽기 ① ② ③ ④ ⑤

   ____

6. **Please show us your license and reservation number.** 면허증과 예약번호를 보여주세요.
   따라 읽기 ① ② ③ ④ ⑤

MINI DIALOGUE

우리말 부분을 영어로 적고 대화를 익혀 보세요.

1.

2.

호텔 체크인
Hotel Check-in

SENTENCE PRACTICE

배운 표현을 5번 크게 읽고 빈칸에 써보세요.

1. You have a double suite for three nights. 더블 스위트룸을 3일간 예약하셨네요.

따라 읽기 ① ② ③ ④ ⑤

2. You have a triple room for two nights. 트리플 룸을 2일간 예약하셨네요.

따라 읽기 ① ② ③ ④ ⑤

3. I'll use my debit card. 제 직불 카드를 사용할게요.

따라 읽기 ① ② ③ ④ ⑤

4. I'll use this voucher. 이 상품권을 사용할게요.

따라 읽기 ① ② ③ ④ ⑤

5. Is my room by the pool? 제 방이 수영장 옆인가요?

따라 읽기 ① ② ③ ④ ⑤

6. Is my room facing the city? 제 방이 도시와 마주 보고 있나요?

따라 읽기 ① ② ③ ④ ⑤

MINI DIALOGUE

우리말 부분을 영어로 적고 대화를 익혀 보세요.

1.

2.

DAY 33

호텔 컨시어지
The Hotel Concierge

SENTENCE PRACTICE

한글 문장을 3초 안에 영어로 말하고 영어 문장을 써보세요.

1. 오늘 베를린에 가고 싶어요. I would like to ____.

2. 피사의 사탑을 보고 싶어요. I would like to ____.

3. 포르투갈에서 오셨나요? Are you from ____?

4. 콜롬비아에서 오셨나요? Are you from ____?

5. 오늘 하이킹하실 건가요? Are you going __________________________________ today?

6. 오늘 쇼핑하실 건가요? Are you going __________________________________ today?

7. 2시에 떠나는 게 어때요? Why don't we ____?

8. 드레스덴 대성당부터 가는 게 어때요? Why don't we ____________________________________?

---

go to Berlin today 오늘 베를린에 가다	**see the Leaning Tower of Pisa** 피사의 사탑을 보다
Portugal 포르투갈	**Colombia** 콜롬비아
hiking 하이킹	**shopping** 쇼핑
leave at 2 2시에 떠나다	**go to the Dresden Cathedral first** 드레스덴 대성당부터 가다

MINI DIALOGUE

우리말 부분을 영어로 적고 대화를 익혀 보세요.

1.

2.

SENTENCE PRACTICE

한글 문장을 3초 안에 영어로 말하고 영어 문장을 써보세요.

1. 사진을 찍을 동안 누군가에게 이것을 맡아달라고 합시다.

Let's get someone to ___________________________.

2. 누군가에게 우리 사진을 찍어달라고 합시다.

Let's get someone to ___________________________.

3. 5초만 누르시면 됩니다.

Just ___________________________.

4. 이 버튼을 가볍게 두드리시면 됩니다.

Just ___________________________.

5. 저 동상이 사진에 나오게 찍어 주시겠어요?

Could you get ___________________________?

6. 저 계단도 나오게 찍어주시겠어요?

Could you get ___________________________ as well?

7. 오른쪽으로 조금만 움직이시겠어요?

Can you move ___________________________?

8. 뒤로 한발만 움직이시겠어요?

Can you move ___________________________?

---

hold this while we take a picture 사진 찍을 동안 맡다

hold this down for five seconds 5초간 누르다

the statue in the picture 저 동상이 사진 안에

a little to the right 오른쪽으로 조금

take a picture of us 우리 사진을 찍다

tap this button 버튼을 가볍게 두드리다

the stairs in it 저 계단이 안에

back a step 한발 뒤로

MINI DIALOGUE

우리말 부분을 영어로 적고 대화를 익혀 보세요.

1.

2.

DAY 35

호텔 체크아웃
Hotel Check-out

배운 표현을 5번 크게 읽고 빈칸에 써보세요.

1. I'd like to return my keys. 열쇠를 반납하고 싶은데요.

따라 읽기 ① ② ③ ④ ⑤

____

2. I'd like to store my bags here for the day. 오늘 가방을 여기 두고 싶은데요.

따라 읽기 ① ② ③ ④ ⑤

____

3. Kim returns the kettle. Kim은 주전자를 반납한다.

따라 읽기 ① ② ③ ④ ⑤

____

4. Kim returns the umbrella. Kim은 우산을 반납한다.

따라 읽기 ① ② ③ ④ ⑤

____

5. Thank you for staying here. 여기 머물러주셔서 감사합니다.

따라 읽기 ① ② ③ ④ ⑤

____

6. Thank you for staying at the Grand Hotel. 그랜드 호텔에 머물러주셔서 감사합니다.

따라 읽기 ① ② ③ ④ ⑤

____

우리말 부분을 영어로 적고 대화를 익혀 보세요.

1.

2.

SECTION
8
Health
건강 챙기기

DAY 36

운동
Exercise

SENTENCE PRACTICE

한글 문장을 3초 안에 영어로 말하고 영어 문장을 써보세요.

1. 얼마나 자주 달리기하러 가세요?　　How often do you ______?

2. 얼마나 자주 요가 하세요?　　How often do you ______?

3. 매일 가려고 해요.　　I try to ______.

4. 아침마다 운동하려고 해요.　　I try to ______.

5. 그래서 요가를 좋아합니다.　　That's why ______.

6. 그래서 밤에 운동합니다.　　That's why ______.

7. 얼마나 줌바를 하셨어요?　　How long have you been ______?

8. 얼마나 수업 후에 운동하셨어요?　　How long have you been ______?

go running 달리기하러 가다	**do yoga** 요가 하다
go every day 매일 가다	**exercise in the mornings** 아침마다 운동하다
I like yoga 요가를 좋아하다	**I exercise at night** 밤에 운동하다
doing Zumba 줌바를 하다	**working out after class** 수업 후에 운동하다

MINI DIALOGUE

우리말 부분을 영어로 적고 대화를 익혀 보세요.

1.

2.

DAY 37

사고
An Accident

SENTENCE PRACTICE

다양한 상황에서 표현을 연습하세요.

1. I think I broke my arm.

sprained my ankle 발목을 삐다	**hurt my arm** 팔을 다치다
twisted my wrist 손목이 비틀리다	**threw out my back** 허리를 삐다

2. Can you move your arm?

your hand 당신의 손	**your back** 당신의 허리
your leg 당신의 다리	**your neck** 당신의 목

3. I don't think it's serious.

it's twisted 비틀리다	**it is sprained** 삐다
it will need a cast 깁스가 필요하다	**you need to see a doctor** 병원에 가봐야 하다

4. I'll get your bag.

your things 당신의 물건들	**the doctor** 의사
your stuff 당신의 소지품	**your mom** 당신의 엄마

MINI DIALOGUE

우리말 부분을 영어로 적고 대화를 익혀 보세요.

1.

2.

DAY 38

병원에서
In the Doctor's Office

SENTENCE PRACTICE

배운 표현을 5번 크게 읽고 빈칸에 써보세요.

1. **May I see your prescription?** 처방전을 보여주시겠어요?

   따라 읽기 1 2 3 4 5

   ____

2. **May I see your reservation number?** 예약번호를 보여주시겠어요?

   따라 읽기 1 2 3 4 5

   ____

3. **Mary hands over her chart.** Mary는 차트를 건넨다.

   따라 읽기 1 2 3 4 5

   ____

4. **Henry hands over a pill bottle.** Henry는 약통을 건넨다.

   따라 읽기 1 2 3 4 5

   ____

5. **The nurse points to a sign.** 간호사가 표지판을 가리킨다.

   따라 읽기 1 2 3 4 5

   ____

6. **The doctor points to a chair.** 의사가 의자를 가리킨다.

   따라 읽기 1 2 3 4 5

   ____

MINI DIALOGUE

우리말 부분을 영어로 적고 대화를 익혀 보세요.

1

2.

DAY 39

진찰
The Examination

SENTENCE PRACTICE

배운 표현을 5번 크게 읽고 빈칸에 써보세요.

1. I have the flu. 감기에 걸린 것 같아요.

따라 읽기 ① ② ③ ④ ⑤

____

2. I have a sore throat. 목이 아파요.

따라 읽기 ① ② ③ ④ ⑤

____

3. Dr. Walters looks into George's eye. Walters 박사는 George의 눈을 살펴본다.

따라 읽기 ① ② ③ ④ ⑤

____

4. Dr. Bolton looks into Sally's wound. Bolton 박사는 Sally의 상처를 살펴본다.

따라 읽기 ① ② ③ ④ ⑤

____

5. You need to stay off your feet. 발을 사용하지 마세요.

따라 읽기 ① ② ③ ④ ⑤

____

6. You need to get lots of rest. 많이 쉬셔야겠어요.

따라 읽기 ① ② ③ ④ ⑤

____

MINI DIALOGUE

우리말 부분을 영어로 적고 대화를 익혀 보세요.

1.

2.

DAY 40

약국에서
At the Pharmacy

SENTENCE PRACTICE

한글 문장을 3초 안에 영어로 말하고 영어 문장을 써보세요.

1. 새로운 처방전을 받고 싶습니다.　　**I'd like to get** _______________________.

2. 알레르기약을 받고 싶습니다.　　**I'd like to get** _______________________.

3. Charles는 그의 이름이 불리기를 기다린다.　　**Charles waits for** _______________________.

4. Dorothy는 그녀의 약을 기다린다.　　**Dorothy waits for** _______________________.

5. 자기 전에 이 약을 드세요.　　**You should take** _______________________.

6. 4시간마다 이 약을 드세요.　　**You should take** _______________________.

7. 복부 통증이 있을 수도 있어요.　　**You may have some** _______________________.

8. 짜증이 날 수 있어요.　　**You may have some** _______________________.

a new prescription 새로운 처방전	**some allergy medicine** 알레르기약
his name to be called 그의 이름이 불리다	**her medicine** 그녀의 약
this capsule before sleeping 자기 전에 이 약	**this medicine every four hours** 4시간마다 이 약
stomach pain 복부 통증	**irritability** 짜증

MINI DIALOGUE

우리말 부분을 영어로 적고 대화를 익혀 보세요.

1.

2.

SECTION

9

Special Occasions

특별한 날

DAY 41

파티 계획 짜기
Planning a Party

SENTENCE PRACTICE

다양한 상황에서 표현을 연습하세요.

1. Do you have plans next Tuesday**?**

next month 다음 달	**Tuesday, the 19th** 19일 화요일
next weekend 다음 주말	**this Friday night** 다음 금요일 저녁

2. I want to have a party for my mother's birthday**.**

a get-together 모임	**for my 20th birthday** 나의 20번째 생일
a gathering 모임	**for my graduation party** 나의 졸업 파티

3. I'll make nachos**.**

a spinach dip 시금치 소스	**a cheese cake** 치즈 케이크
a pie 파이	**some cookies** 쿠키

4. Jan **decides to** bring a friend**.**

My husband 내 남편	**book a table at a restaurant** 식당에 테이블을 예약하다
My father 우리 아빠	**invite a friend** 친구를 초대하다

MINI DIALOGUE

우리말 부분을 영어로 적고 대화를 익혀 보세요.

1.

2.

DAY 42

다른 계획
Other Plans

SENTENCE PRACTICE

한글 문장을 3초 안에 영어로 말하고 영어 문장을 써보세요.

1. 오늘 밤 파티에 대해 들었어요?　　**Did you hear about** _______________________?

2. 작년 파티에 대해 들었어요?　　**Did you hear about** _______________________?

3. 조부모님을 만나러 가야 해요.　　**I have to go** _______________________.

4. 시외로 며칠 나가야 해요.　　**I have to go** _______________________.

5. Kyle은 Marge에게 병을 건넨다.　　**Kyle gives** _______________________ **to Marge.**

6. Zheng은 Lucy에게 접시를 건넨다.　　**Zheng gives** _______________________ **to Lucy.**

7. 졸업식 잘하시길 바랍니다!　　**Good luck with** _______________________!

8. 새 직장에서 행운을 빕니다.　　**Good luck with** _______________________!

the party tonight 오늘 밤 파티	**last year's party** 작년 파티
see my grandparents 조부모님을 만나다	**out of town for a couple of days** 시외로 며칠
a bottle 병	**a plate** 접시
your graduation 당신의 졸업식	**your new job** 당신의 새 직장

MINI DIALOGUE

우리말 부분을 영어로 적고 대화를 익혀 보세요.

1.

2.

DAY 43

파티 준비
Party Preparation

SENTENCE PRACTICE

다양한 상황에서 표현을 연습하세요.

1. Did you bring the banners**?**

the candles 초	**the cake** 케이크
the balloons 풍선	**the snacks** 간식

2. I brought some party favors**.**

some presents 선물 몇 개	**a gift for you** 당신을 위한 선물
some food 음식 약간	**some games to play** 할 게임

3. Dad is preparing the party in the back yard**.**

pool 수영장	**out back** 뒤쪽에
barbecue 바비큐 파티	**out front** 앞쪽에

4. Could you help me with this pot**?**

this table 이 테이블	**the food** 음식
the silverware 은 식기류	**the decorations** 장식

MINI DIALOGUE

우리말 부분을 영어로 적고 대화를 익혀 보세요.

1.

2.

DAY 44

선물 포장하기
Wrapping a Gift

SENTENCE PRACTICE

다양한 상황에서 표현을 연습하세요.

1. I got my sister some earrings**.**

my mother 우리 엄마	**a new bag** 새 가방
my brother 내 남동생	**a DVD** DVD

2. I got it for $100**.**

a silly price 말도 안 되는 가격	**40% off** 40% 할인
a bargain 특가	**only $10** 단 10달러

3. Gift bags **are on sale.**

Shirts 셔츠	**All wood products** 모든 목공품
Some shoes 몇몇 신발	**Gift sets** 선물 세트

4. When does this deal **end?**

this special sale 이 특별 할인	**the going-out-of-business sale** 점포 정리 세일
the annual event 연례행사	**this sales event** 이 할인 행사

MINI DIALOGUE

우리말 부분을 영어로 적고 대화를 익혀 보세요.

1.

2.

DAY 45

파티에서
At the Party

SENTENCE PRACTICE

대화를 보고 빈칸을 채워보세요.

1. **A Did you ___________________ this pie?**
   이 파이를 만들었어요?

   B No, my mother did.
   아니요, 우리 엄마가 만들었어요.

2. **A ___________________ this ___________________?**
   이 식사를 만들었어요?

   B Yes, I'm very proud of it!
   네, 너무 자랑스러워요!

3. **A Don't ___________________ to blow out the candles.**
   초 부는 거 잊지 마세요.

   B Oh, that's right!
   오, 맞아요!

4. **A ___________________ say goodbye to all the guests.**
   모든 손님들에게 작별 인사하는 거 잊지 마세요.

   B I just finished.
   방금 다 했어요.

make 만들다	**meal** 식사	**forget** 잊다

MINI DIALOGUE

우리말 부분을 영어로 적고 대화를 익혀 보세요.

1.

2.

SECTION

10

Descriptions

묘사하기

DAY 46

이발하기
Getting a Haircut

SENTENCE PRACTICE

배운 표현을 5번 크게 읽고 빈칸에 써보세요.

1. **Just trim the ends, please.** 그냥 끝부분만 다듬어 주세요.

   따라 읽기 ① ② ③ ④ ⑤

   ____

2. **Just give me a buzz cut, please.** 그냥 아주 짧게 잘라주세요.

   따라 읽기 ① ② ③ ④ ⑤

   ____

3. **Do you live in Mexico City?** 멕시코 시티에 사시나요?

   따라 읽기 ① ② ③ ④ ⑤

   ____

4. **Do you live in Toronto?** 토론토에 사시나요?

   따라 읽기 ① ② ③ ④ ⑤

   ____

5. **Do you want me to style your hair?** 머리 스타일링을 해드릴까요?

   따라 읽기 ① ② ③ ④ ⑤

   ____

6. **Do you want me to dry your hair?** 머리 말려드릴까요?

   따라 읽기 ① ② ③ ④ ⑤

   ____

MINI DIALOGUE

우리말 부분을 영어로 적고 대화를 익혀 보세요.

1.

2.

DAY 47

분실물
Lost and Found

SENTENCE PRACTICE

한글 문장을 3초 안에 영어로 말하고 영어 문장을 써보세요.

1. 열차에 제 핸드폰을 놓고 간 것 같아요.

I think I left ________________________.

2. 거기에 제 지갑을 놓고 간 것 같아요.

I think I left ________________________.

3. 지갑에 무엇이 들어있나요?

What was in ________________________?

4. 그 가방에 무엇이 들어있나요?

What was in ________________________?

5. 제 핸드폰과 열쇠들, 그리고 지갑이 있었어요.

It had ____________, ____________, and ____________ in it.

6. 제가 가장 좋아하는 목걸이와 돈 전부, 신용카드가 있었어요.

It had ____________, ____________, and ____________ in it.

7. 당신의 이메일 주소를 알려주실래요?

Can I have your ________________________, please?

8. 당신의 주소를 알려주실래요?

Can I have your ________________________, please?

my cell phone on the train 열차에 내 핸드폰	**my purse there** 그곳에 내 지갑
the purse 지갑	**that bag** 그 가방
my cell phone 내 핸드폰	**my keys** 내 열쇠들
my wallet 내 지갑	**my favorite necklace** 가장 좋아하는 목걸이
all my money 돈 전부	**a credit card** 신용카드
email address 이메일 주소	**address** 주소

MINI DIALOGUE

우리말 부분을 영어로 적고 대화를 익혀 보세요.

1.

2.

DAY 48

요리 실습
A Cooking Lesson

SENTENCE PRACTICE

다양한 상황에서 표현을 연습하세요.

1. What are we making today?

learning 배우는	**studying** 공부하는
doing 하는	**baking today** 오늘 굽는

2. How much salt do we need?

oil 기름	**baking soda** 베이킹소다
flour 밀가루	**basil** 바질

3. They look undercooked.

fresh 신선한	**tasty** 맛있는
greasy 기름진	**crispy** 바삭한

4. Evan takes the plate out of the cabinet.

a dish 접시	**cupboard** 찬장
a bowl 그릇	**kitchen** 부엌

MINI DIALOGUE

우리말 부분을 영어로 적고 대화를 익혀 보세요.

1.

2.

DAY 49

데이트
The Date

SENTENCE PRACTICE

한글 문장을 3초 안에 영어로 말하고 영어 문장을 써보세요.

1. 지난번엔 뭐 했나요?　　　　　　　　**What did you do** _______________________?

2. 지난주에 뭐 했나요?　　　　　　　　**What did you do** _______________________?

3. 시내에 있는 케이크 가게에 갔어요.　　**We went to** _______________________.

4. 중국 식당에 갔어요.　　　　　　　　**We went to** _______________________.

5. Danny는 어떻게 생겼어요?　　　　　**What does** _______________________ **look like?**

6. 당신의 여자친구는 어떻게 생겼어요?　**What does** _______________________ **look like?**

7. 그녀는 금발이고 초록색 눈을 가졌어요.　**She has** _______________ **and** _______________.

8. 그는 황갈색 피부에 까만 눈을 가졌어요.　**He has** _______________ **and** _______________.

---

last time 지난번	**last week** 지난주
a cake shop in the city 시내에 있는 케이크 가게	**a Chinese restaurant** 중국 식당
Danny Danny	**your girlfriend** 당신의 여자친구
blonde hair 금발	**green eyes** 초록색 눈
tan skin 황갈색 피부	**dark eyes** 까만 눈

MINI DIALOGUE

우리말 부분을 영어로 적고 대화를 익혀 보세요.

1.

2.

DAY 50

영화 얘기
A Movie Discussion

SENTENCE PRACTICE

다양한 상황에서 표현을 연습하세요.

1. What are you doing next weekend**?**

next week 다음 주	**next Monday** 다음 주 월요일
this Friday 이번 금요일	**on Saturday** 토요일에

2. Janet and I **are going to** see a musical**.**

We 우리	**watch a film** 영화를 보다
My boyfriend and I 나와 내 남자친구	**get dinner** 저녁을 먹다

3. How did you like the music**?**

the show 그 쇼	**the prequel** 전편
the performance 공연	**the cinematography** 촬영술

4. I like Tom Holland **the best.**

Ryan Reynolds Ryan Reynolds	**Hugh Jackman** Hugh Jackman
Drew Barrymore Drew Barrymore	**Audrey Hepburn** Audrey Hepburn

MINI DIALOGUE

우리말 부분을 영어로 적고 대화를 익혀 보세요.

1.

2.

ANSWER KEY

DAY 1 Introductions

MINI DIALOGUE

1. hometown
2. plans

DAY 2 The Visit

SENTENCE PRACTICE

1. calling
2. helping
3. your hat
4. your bags
5. the kitchen
6. the office
7. a drink
8. something to eat

MINI DIALOGUE

1. inviting
2. jacket

DAY 3 Occupations

MINI DIALOGUE

1. work for
2. a new job

DAY 4 School

MINI DIALOGUE

1. major
2. sophomore

DAY 5 Saying Goodbye

SENTENCE PRACTICE

1. some water
2. a blanket
3. a new fork
4. some paper
5. nice, meet
6. nice, talk
7. you have time In the afternoon
8. Theo can come over

MINI DIALOGUE

1. night owls
2. jar

DAY 6 Women's Clothing

MINI DIALOGUE

1. spring clothes
2. How about, medium one

DAY 7 Sizes and Trying Things On

MINI DIALOGUE

1. fit better
2. popular

DAY 8 Men's Clothing

SENTENCE PRACTICE

1. a shirt
2. some socks
3. style, sweater
4. kind, jacket
5. denim shirts
6. silk skirts
7. two of those
8. the bigger one

MINI DIALOGUE

1. I need
2. have a sale

DAY 9 Paying at the Counter

SENTENCE PRACTICE

1. $9.50
2. $7,390.90
3. this coupon
4. a credit card
5. your card
6. your coupon
7. call us
8. exchange this for a bigger size, bring it back

MINI DIALOGUE

1. cash or card
2. exchange

DAY 10 Electronics

MINI DIALOGUE

1. best model, expensive
2. warranty

DAY 11 At a Fast Food Restaurant

SENTENCE PRACTICE

1. have
2. eat
3. some more water
4. an extra napkin
5. some plates
6. some mayonnaise
7. burger
8. meal

MINI DIALOGUE

1. order
2. ketchup

DAY 12 At the Movies

SENTENCE PRACTICE

1. romance movie
2. action film
3. *Die Tomorrow*
4. *Blue Skies*

MINI DIALOGUE

1. large popcorn
2. seats

DAY 13 Helping a Neighbor

MATCHING

1. grandchildren
2. neighbor

DAY 14   At a Coffee Shop

1. Happy Coffee
2. Home Palace
3. a hot chocolate
4. a small decaf
5. sugar and milk
6. a gift card
7. a hot cappuccino
8. some creams

1. welcome to
2. low-fat

DAY 15   At the Museum

1. taxi
2. sculpture

DAY 16   Taking a Taxi

1. want to
2. near

DAY 17   In the Library

1. romances
2. biographies
3. *The Bluebird*
4. *On the Hills*
5. artist
6. mystery writer
7. the poem
8. *Burning House*

1. kind of books
2. thrillers

DAY 18   Taking a Bus

1. often, every 10 minutes
2. many stops

DAY 19   Getting Gas

1. gas station
2. cover

DAY 20   Asking for Directions

1. know, ask for directions
2. no idea

DAY 21   Arriving at the Restaurant

1. window
2. waiter

DAY 22   Ordering Drinks and an Appetizer

1. lemonade
2. calamari

DAY 23   The Waiter Returns

1. for dessert
2. to go
3. your beans
4. your potatoes
5. veggie, chicken, shrimp
6. mozzarella, pepper jack, cheddar
7. club sandwich
8. chef's salad

1. Medium rare
2. seafood spaghetti

DAY 24   The Food Arrives

1. your food
2. your drink
3. too cold
4. just right
5. an extra plate
6. something else to drink
7. your empty glasses
8. those plates

1. Would you like
2. away

DAY 25   A Lovely Meal

1. dessert
2. excellent

DAY 26   Check-in

1. passport and ticket
2. attach

DAY 27   Security

1. empty
2. headaches

DAY 28 Boarding

SENTENCE PRACTICE

1. for flight 309 to Paris
2. all rows
3. put this bag away for you
4. get you a seat belt extender
5. put this under my seat
6. put this underneath my seat
7. all electronic devices are turned off
8. all trays are put away

MINI DIALOGUE

1. get by
2. make sure

DAY 29 The Flight

MINI DIALOGUE

1. on business, on vacation
2. landing

DAY 30 Immigration (Arrival)

SENTENCE PRACTICE

1. Rome
2. Brussels
3. visiting family
4. here
5. two days
6. the next two months
7. on some family business
8. seeing a friend

MINI DIALOGUE

1. arrival card
2. purpose

DAY 31 Car Rental

MINI DIALOGUE

1. international driver's license
2. free map

DAY 32 Hotel Check-in

MINI DIALOGUE

1. single room
2. credit card

DAY 33 The Hotel Concierge

MINI DIALOGUE

1. go to Berlin today
2. see the Leaning Tower of Pisa
3. Portugal
4. Colombia
5. hiking
6. shopping
7. leave at 2
8. go to the Dresden Cathedral first

MINI DIALOGUE

1. sightseeing
2. have a car

DAY 34 Sightseeing

SENTENCE PRACTICE

1. hold this while we take a picture
2. take a picture of us
3. hold this down for five seconds
4. tap this button
5. the statue in the picture
6. the stairs in it
7. a little to the right
8. back a step

MINI DIALOGUE

1. background
2. Smile

DAY 35 Hotel Check-out

MINI DIALOGUE

1. mini-bar
2. charge

DAY 36 Exercise

SENTENCE PRACTICE

1. go running
2. do yoga
3. go every day
4. exercise in the mornings
5. I like yoga
6. I exercise at night
7. doing Zumba
8. working out after class

MINI DIALOGUE

1. work out
2. volleyball, basketball

DAY 37 An Accident

MINI DIALOGUE

1. happened, balance
2. move it

DAY 38 In the Doctor's Office

MINI DIALOGUE

1. have an appointment
2. bad cold, wrist

DAY 39 The Examination

MINI DIALOGUE

1. trouble
2. breathe deeply

DAY 40 At the Pharmacy

1. a new prescription
2. some allergy medicine
3. his name to be called
4. her medicine
5. this capsule before sleeping
6. this medicine every four hours
7. stomach pain
8. irritability

1. have a seat
2. side effects, stomach

DAY 41 Planning a Party

1. have a party
2. buy a cake, bake

DAY 42 Other Plans

1. the party tonight
2. last year's party
3. see my grandparents
4. out of town for a couple of days
5. a bottle
6. a plate
7. your graduation
8. your new job

1. hear about
2. Don't mention it

DAY 43 Party Preparation

1. in the kitchen
2. ceiling

DAY 44 Wrapping a Gift

1. vase
2. How much did it cost

DAY 45 At the Party

1. make
2. Did you make, meal
3. forget
4. Don't forget to

1. make a wish
2. sculpture, glad

DAY 46 Getting a Haircut

1. wash your hair
2. owe

DAY 47 Lost and Found

1. my cell phone on the train
2. my purse there
3. the purse
4. that bag
5. my cell phone, my keys, my wallet
6. my favorite necklace, all my money, a credit card
7. email address
8. address

1. brand
2. nylon, canvas straps

DAY 48 A Cooking Lesson

1. grate
2. chop up

DAY 49 The Date

1. last time
2. last week
3. a cake shop in the city
4. a Chinese restaurant
5. Danny
6. your girlfriend
7. blonde hair, green eyes
8. tan skin, dark eyes

1. by the river
2. hit it off

DAY 50 A Movie Discussion

1. sci-fi movies
2. special effects